Knitting Wheel Fashions

Yes, you can knit *without using needles*! Let a knitting wheel hold your work while you create hats, belts, scarves, handbags, and so much more. It's so simple, even a child can do it. And since there are no slippery needles to grip, the knitting wheel is the perfect creative tool for anyone whose fingers are sometimes stiff or painful.

We'll show you how to use the round wheel and the straight wheel to create beautiful knitted fabric. Just follow the easy instructions that begin on page 22. You'll soon finish a mohair evening bag, a "fur" wrap, a warm shrug, or any of fourteen fun, fast, and fabulous accessories.

KNITTING WHEELS

The **round wheel**, also known as a knitting wheel, loom, spool, and reel, can be made out of nylon, wood, or plastic. Round wheels come in many sizes. We used four sizes for our projects: Small with 24 pegs, Medium with 31 pegs, Large with 36 pegs, and Extra Large with 41 pegs.

The round wheels can be used to make a tubular piece excellent for hats and purses, and also a flat piece great for belts, wraps, shawls, and shrugs. All of our patterns are worked in a Raised Crossed Stitch for better elastic action, also known as Crossed Stocking Stitch.

The **straight wheel**, also known as a knitting board, straight loom, rectangle loom, and infinity rake, can be made out of nylon or wood. The straight wheel comes in different lengths ranging from 12" to 60" (30.5 cm to 152.5 cm) long and can be used for a variety of projects. We used a 15" (38 cm) straight wheel that has 36 pegs in 18 pairs and a side peg on each end used to anchor the yarn during work. Thick, flat, double-sided reversible knitting (ribbing) can be produced on the straight wheel – super for scarves that won't curl.

Our designers used the Knifty Knitter™ from Provo Craft®.

KNITTING WHEEL TOOL

Some wheels come with a special tool that is used to help you lift the bottom loop on each peg over the top loop. The tool can also be purchased separately. A yarn needle, knitting needle, and even a nut pick can be used for the tool.

CROCHET HOOK

Some of the projects require a crochet hook to work the bind off row and/or fringe. Use size K (6.5 mm) or any size large enough to catch both strands of yarn.

YARN

The projects included are made holding 2 or 3 strands of yarn together. This is a terrific way to achieve wonderful results combining some of the specialty yarns available.

> *Tip*   Wheel knitting will be easier to learn if you use a smooth yarn, as the stitches will be clearly visible.

1. Neck Cuff & Belt

EASY

MATERIALS

- Super Bulky Weight Yarn **SUPER BULKY 6**
  [3 ounces, 115 yards (85 grams, 105 meters) per skein]:
  White/Black - 1 skein
- Medium Weight Yarn **MEDIUM 4**
  [7 ounces, 364 yards (198 grams, 333 meters) per skein]:
  Black - 1 skein
- 24 and 41 Peg round wheels
- Knitting wheel tool
- Crochet hook
- Yarn needle
- ½" (12 mm) Gold sequins with large hole - 1 package
  (A hole punch can be used to make the hole large enough for yarn to go through.)

NECK CUFF

Using 41 peg wheel and holding one strand of each color together, make a tubular piece 10" (25.5 cm) long **(see Tubular Knitting, page 22)**.

To form Neck Cuff, lift up bottom edge toward inside of wheel and place loops from first row over pegs **(Fig. 5, page 26)**. Lift the bottom loop on each peg over the top loop and off the peg. Cut White/Black yarn.

To work chain 2 bind off, insert crochet hook in loop on last peg and lift it off the peg, working to your left, insert hook in loop on next peg, lift it off the peg and pull it through loop on hook **(Fig. 8a, page 27)**, using Black, chain 2 **(Fig. 13, page 30)**, ★ insert hook in loop on next peg, lift it off the peg and pull it through loop on hook, chain 2; repeat from ★ until all of the loops have been removed from the wheel and there is one loop on crochet hook. Insert hook in first stitch, yarn over hook and pull through stitch and loop on hook, cut yarn and pull end through final loop **(Fig. 8c, page 27)**.

Weave in all yarn ends between layers of Neck Cuff.

BELT

Using 24 peg wheel and holding one strand of each color together, make a flat piece on 5 pegs 52" (132 cm) long **(see Flat Knitting, page 24)**.

To work chain 1 bind off, insert crochet hook in loop on last peg and lift it off the peg, working to your left, insert hook in loop on next peg, lift it off the peg and pull it through loop on hook **(Fig. 8a, page 27)**, ★ chain 1 **(Fig. 13, page 30)**, insert hook in loop on next peg, lift it off the peg and pull it through loop on hook; repeat from ★ until all of the loops have been removed from the wheel and there is one loop on crochet hook. Cut yarn and pull end through final loop **(Fig. 8c, page 27)**.

FRINGE

Cut a piece of cardboard 3" x 11" (7.5 cm x 28 cm). Holding one strand of each color together, wind the yarns **loosely** and **evenly** lengthwise around the cardboard until the card is filled, then cut across one end; repeat as needed.

Neck Cuff: Using photo as a guide for placement, choose one vertical row of stitches across the width of Cuff. Holding one strand of each color together and using a crochet hook, pull end of strands through a stitch. Tie strands in a square knot to secure. Repeat, spacing as desired.

Belt: Hold 2 strands of each color together; fold in half. With **wrong** side of one end facing and using a crochet hook, draw the folded end up through a stitch and pull the loose ends through the folded end; draw the knot up **tightly** **(Figs. 16a & b, page 31)**. Repeat, spacing as desired.

Both: Thread each end of fringe through a sequin and tie in a knot to secure.

Design by Cathy Lowry.

Ear Warmer

EASY

MATERIALS

- Bulky Weight Brushed Acrylic Yarn **BULKY 5**
  [3½ ounces, 142 yards
   (100 grams, 129 meters) per skein]:
     Blue - 1 skein
- Medium Weight Yarn **MEDIUM 4**
  [2½ ounces, 120 yards
   (70 grams, 110 meters) per skein]:
     White - 1 skein
- 36 Peg round wheel
- Knitting wheel tool
- Crochet hook
- Yarn needle

BODY

Holding one strand of each color together, make a tubular piece 8″ (20.5 cm) long **(see Tubular Knitting, page 22)**.

To form Ear Warmer, lift up bottom edge toward inside of wheel and place loops from first row over pegs **(Fig. 5, page 26)**. Lift the bottom loop on each peg over the top loop and off the peg. Cut White.

To work chain 1 bind off, insert crochet hook in loop on last peg and lift it off the peg, working to your left, insert hook in loop on next peg, lift it off the peg and pull it through loop on hook **(Fig. 8a, page 27)**, using Blue, chain 1 **(Fig. 13, page 30)**, ★ insert hook in loop on next peg, lift it off the peg and pull it through loop on hook, chain 1; repeat from ★ until all of the loops have been removed from the wheel and there is one loop on crochet hook. Insert hook in first stitch, yarn over hook and pull through stitch and loop on hook, cut yarn and pull end through final loop **(Fig. 8c, page 27)**.

Weave in all yarn ends between layers of Ear Warmer.

Design by Cathy Lowry.

Basic Hat

Shown on page 6.

◼◼◻◻ **EASY**

MATERIALS

- Medium Weight Yarn **MEDIUM 4**
  [7 ounces, 364 yards (198 grams, 333 meters) per skein]:
    Black - 1 skein
  [6 ounces, 316 yards
  (170 grams, 289 meters) per skein]:
    Black/Gold - 1 skein
- 36 Peg round wheel
- Knitting wheel tool
- Yarn needle

CUFF

Holding 2 strands of Black together (pull one strand from center and one from the outside), make a tubular piece 3" (7.5 cm) long **(see Tubular Knitting, page 22)**.

To form Cuff, lift up bottom edge toward inside of wheel and place loops from first row over pegs **(Fig. 5, page 26)**. Lift the bottom loop on each peg over the top loop and off the peg.

BODY

Row 1: Add one strand of Black/Gold to the 2 strands of Black and work one row.

Rows 2-12 (Double wrap row)**:** Wrap each peg twice on wrapping row, and complete knit stitches by lifting bottom loop on each peg over the two new wraps and off the peg **(Figs. 7a & b, pages 26 and 27)**. Lift each top wrap off the peg, making loose stitches **(Fig. 7c, page 27)** and pull work down from the inside to keep loops from slipping off the pegs.

Rows 13 and 14: Cut one strand of Black and work two single wrap rows using one strand of each color.

Row 15 (Decrease row)**:** Lift loop from first peg and place it on the second peg. Lift loop from the third peg and place it on the fourth peg. Continue around until you have 2 loops on every other peg. Lift the bottom loop on each peg over the top loop and off the peg. There will be one loop on every other peg.

Cut yarn leaving a 24" (61 cm) end. Thread yarn needle with end. Beginning with the last peg, insert yarn needle in each loop and lift it off the peg **(Fig. 6a, page 26)**. With yarn to inside of Hat, pull the end tightly gathering the loops to the center of the tube **(Fig. 6b, page 26)**; knot yarn tightly and weave in the end; clip end close to work.

Using Black, make pom-pom **(Figs. 17a-c, page 31)** and attach to top of Hat.

Design by Charlene G. Finiello.

Sequined Hat

◖■◻▭ EASY

MATERIALS

- Bulky Weight Yarn **BULKY 5**
  [3 ounces, 135 yards (85 grams, 123 meters)
  per skein]:
    Color A - 1 skein
- Super Bulky Weight Short Eyelash Yarn **SUPER BULKY 6**
  [1¾ ounces, 47 yards
  (50 grams, 43 meters) per skein]:
    Color B - 1 skein
- Effect Yarn with gold sequins
  [60 yards (55 meters) per ball]:
    Color C - 1 ball
- 36 Peg round wheel
- Knitting wheel tool
- Yarn needle

BAND

Holding 2 strands of Color A together (pull one strand
from center and one from the outside), make a tubular
piece 3" (7.5 cm) long **(see Tubular Knitting,
page 22)**. Piece will roll up to form Band. Cut yarn.

BODY

Row 1: Holding 2 strands of Color B and one strand
of Color C together, work one row.

Row 2 (Double wrap row)**:** Wrap each peg twice
on wrapping row, and complete knit stitches by lifting
bottom loop on each peg over the two new wraps
and off the peg **(Figs. 7a & b, pages 26 and 27)**.
Lift each top wrap off the peg, making loose stitches
(Fig. 7c, page 27) and pull work down from the inside
to keep loops from slipping off the pegs.

Repeat Row 2 for 5" (12.5 cm).

Cut one strand of Color B. Work 1" (2.5 cm) in single
wrap.

Last Row (Decrease row)**:** Lift loop from first peg and
place it on the second peg. Lift loop from the third peg
and place it on the fourth peg. Continue around until
you have 2 loops on every other peg. Lift the bottom
loop on each peg over the top loop and off the peg.
There will be one loop on every other peg.

Cut yarn leaving a 24" (61 cm) end. Thread yarn
needle with end. Beginning with the last peg, insert
yarn needle in each loop and lift it off the peg
(Fig. 6a, page 26). With yarn to inside of Hat, pull the
end tightly gathering the loops to the center of the tube
(Fig. 6b, page 26); knot yarn tightly and weave in the
end; clip end close to work.

Design by Cathy Lowry.

5. *Spiral Hat*

Shown on page 7.

■■■□ INTERMEDIATE

MATERIALS
- Medium Weight Yarn **MEDIUM 4**
  [7 ounces, 364 yards (198 grams, 333 meters) per skein]:
     Black - 1 skein
  [2¹/₂ ounces, 162 yards (70 grams, 146 meters) per skein]:
     White - 1 skein
- 36 Peg round wheel
- Knitting wheel tool
- Yarn needle

CUFF

Holding 2 strands of Black together (pull one strand from center and one from the outside), make a tubular piece 4" (10 cm) long **(see Tubular Knitting, page 22)**.

To form Cuff, lift up bottom edge toward inside of wheel and place loops from first row over pegs **(Fig. 5, page 26)**. Lift the bottom loop on each peg over the top loop and off the peg. Do **not** cut Black.

BODY

Holding 2 strands of White together, anchor ends.

Row 1: Using White, wrap the first peg, skip 2 pegs, (wrap next peg, skip 2 pegs) around; drop White. Using Black, wrap all skipped pegs. Complete knit stitches.

Row 2: Using White, skip the first peg, wrap the next peg, (skip 2 pegs, wrap next peg) around to last peg, skip last peg; drop White. Using Black, wrap all skipped pegs. Complete knit stitches.

Row 3: Using White, skip the first 2 pegs, wrap the next peg, (skip 2 pegs, wrap next peg) around; drop White. Using Black, wrap all skipped pegs. Complete knit stitches.

Repeat Rows 1-3 for spiral pattern, for 5¹/₂" (14 cm).

Cut White.

Next Row: Using Black, work one row.

Last Row (Decrease row): Lift loop from first peg and place it on the second peg. Lift loop from the third peg and place it on the fourth peg. Continue around until you have 2 loops on every other peg. Lift the bottom loop on each peg over the top loop and off the peg. There will be one loop on every other peg.

Cut yarn leaving a 24" (61 cm) end. Thread yarn needle with end. Beginning with the last peg, insert yarn needle in each loop and lift it off the peg **(Fig. 6a, page 26)**. With yarn to inside of Hat, pull the end tightly gathering the loops to the center of the tube **(Fig. 6b, page 26)**; knot yarn tightly and weave in the end; clip end close to work.

Using Black, make pom-pom **(Figs. 17a-c, page 31)** and attach to top of Hat.

Design by Charlene G. Finiello.

6. Shaggy Dog Hat & Scarf

●■□□ **EASY**

MATERIALS

- Bulky Weight Nubby Yarn **BULKY 5**
  [1¾ ounces, 60 yards (50 grams, 55 meters) per skein]:
  - Tan - 2 skeins
- [1¾ ounces, 64 yards (50 grams, 58 meters) per skein]: **BULKY 5**
  - Off-White - 2 skeins
- 36 Peg round wheel for Hat
- 36 Peg straight wheel for Scarf
- Knitting wheel tool
- Yarn needle
- ¾" (19 mm) Bangles (gold and silver) - 50
  (A hole punch can be used to make the hole large enough for yarn to go through.)

HAT

Holding one strand of each color together, make a tubular piece 8½" (21.5 cm) long **(see Tubular Knitting, page 22)**.

Last Row (Decrease row): Lift loop from first peg and place it on the second peg. Lift loop from the third peg and place it on the fourth peg. Continue around until you have 2 loops on every other peg. Lift the bottom loop on each peg over the top loop and off the peg. There will be one loop on every other peg.

Cut yarn leaving a 24" (61 cm) end. Thread yarn needle with end. Beginning with the last peg, insert yarn needle in each loop and lift it off the peg **(Fig. 6a, page 26)**. With yarn to inside of Hat, pull the end tightly gathering the loops to the center of the tube **(Fig. 6b, page 26)**; knot yarn tightly and weave in the end; clip end close to work.

Thread 26 bangles on Off-White, alternating gold and silver. Make pom-pom by winding yarn on a 4" (10 cm) piece of cardboard, pushing a bangle on each side of each wrap **(Figs. 17a-c, page 31)**. Tie center of pom-pom but do **not** cut the loops. Attach pom-pom to top of Hat.

SCARF

Using straight wheel, holding one strand of each color together and leaving a long end of Off-White only for bangle attachment, wrap 7 pairs of pegs and make a piece 47" (119.5 cm) long **(see Straight Wheel, page 28)**.

Work chain 1 bind off **(Figs. 10a & b, page 29)**. Cut Tan. Cut Off-White leaving a long end.

Thread yarn needle with long end. Thread one bangle on yarn, insert needle through end of Scarf, leaving a loop long enough for bangle to dangle. Repeat across, using 12 bangles and alternating gold and silver.

Repeat for second end of Scarf.

Design by Charlene G. Finiello.

7.

Mohair Bag

▰▰▰▱ INTERMEDIATE

MATERIALS

BULKY 5

- Bulky Weight Mohair type Yarn
  [1¾ ounces, 82 yards
  (50 grams, 75 meters) per skein]:
      Variegated - 1 skein
- Super Fine Weight Yarn **SUPER FINE 1**
      Light Brown - 80 yards (73 meters)
- 31 Peg round wheel
- Knitting wheel tool
- Crochet hook
- Yarn needle
- Sewing needle and thread
- Straight pins
- Beaded edging - 8" (20.5 cm) length
- 1" (2.5 cm) Button
- Fabric for lining (optional) - ¼ yard (23 cm)

BODY

Holding one strand of each color together, make a tubular piece 6" (15 cm) long **(see Tubular Knitting, page 22)**.

To work chain 1 bind off on 15 stitches, insert crochet hook in loop on last peg and lift it off the peg, working to your left, ★ insert hook in loop on next peg, lift it off the peg and pull it through loop on hook **(Fig. 8a, page 27)**, chain 1 **(Fig. 13, page 30)**; repeat from ★ until 15 loops remain on pegs. Place loop on hook on next empty peg.

FLAP

Work flat for 3" (7.5 cm) to form flap **(see Flat Knitting, page 24)**.

Work chain 1 bind off for remaining stitches.

FINISHING

Insert ribbon edge of beaded edging into the bottom opening and pin in place. Working through all 3 layers, sew bottom closed.

For Strap, holding one strand of each color together, make a chain 36" (91.5 cm) long **or** to desired length; finish off.
Attach Strap to inside of Bag at each side of Flap.

Fold Flap down and sew button to Body just below Flap.

For Button loop, holding one strand of each color together, make a chain 4" (10 cm) long **or** to desired length; finish off.
Attach loop to inside edge of Flap.

Weave in all yarn ends; clip ends close to work.

Make lining if desired; sew lining to inside top edge of bag.

Design by Cathy Lowry.

Cotton Bag

■■■□ INTERMEDIATE

MATERIALS

- Bulky Weight Cotton Yarn
  [4 ounces, 140 yards
  (113 grams, 128 meters) per skein]:
    1 skein
- 31 Peg round wheel
- Knitting wheel tool
- Crochet hook
- Yarn needle
- Sewing needle and thread
- 1″ (2.5 cm) Button
- Fabric for lining (optional) - ¼ yard (23 cm)

BODY

Holding 2 strands of yarn together (pull one strand from center and one from the outside) and leaving a long end for sewing, make a tubular piece 7½″ (19 cm) long **(see Tubular Knitting, page 22)**.

To work chain 1 bind off on 15 stitches, insert crochet hook in loop on last peg and lift it off the peg, working to your left, ★ insert hook in loop on next peg, lift it off the peg and pull it through loop on hook **(Fig. 8a, page 27)**, chain 1 **(Fig. 13, page 30)**; repeat from ★ until 15 loops remain on pegs. Place loop on hook on next empty peg.

FLAP

Work flat for 3″ (7.5 cm) to form flap **(see Flat Knitting, page 24)**.

Work chain 1 bind off for remaining stitches.

FINISHING

With long end, sew bottom closed.

Bottom Fringe: Holding 2 strands of yarn together and working through **both** thicknesses, join yarn with slip stitch at one side of bottom of Bag **(Fig. 14, page 30)**; (chain 6, slip stitch in next stitch) across; finish off.

For Strap, holding 2 strands of yarn together, make a chain 36″ (91.5 cm) long **or** to desired length; finish off.
Attach Strap to inside of bag at each side of Flap.

Fold Flap down and sew button to Body just below Flap.

For Button loop, holding 2 strands of yarn together, make a chain 4″ (10 cm) long **or** to desired length; finish off.
Attach loop to inside edge of Flap.

Weave in all yarn ends; clip ends close to work.

Make lining if desired; sew lining to inside top edge of bag.

Design by Margaret Gonzales.

Shrug

◼◼◼▢ INTERMEDIATE

Size: **Finished Measurements:**
Small   16" x 51" (40.5 cm x 129.5 cm)
Medium   21" x 55" (53.5 cm x 139.5 cm)
Large   26¹⁄₂" x 58" (67.5 cm x 147.5 cm)

Note: Instructions are written for size Small with sizes Medium and Large in braces { }. Instructions will be easier to read if you circle all the numbers pertaining to your size. If only one number is given, it applies to all sizes.

MATERIALS

- Medium Weight Yarn **[4] MEDIUM**
  [1³⁄₄ ounces, 77 yards
  (50 grams, 71 meters) per skein]:
  Orange - 3 skeins
- Super Bulky Weight Short Eyelash Yarn **[6] SUPER BULKY**
  [1³⁄₄ ounces, 47 yards (50 grams, 43 meters) per skein]:
  Black - 3 skeins
- 41 Peg round wheel
- Knitting wheel tool
- Stitch holder
- Yarn needle

CUFF

Holding two strands of Orange together (pull one strand from center and one from the outside), make a flat piece on 16{18-20} pegs, 6" (15 cm) long *(see Flat Knitting, page 24)*.

To form Cuff, lift up bottom edge toward inside of wheel and place loops from first row over pegs *(Fig. 5, page 26)*. Lift the bottom loop on each peg over the top loop and off the peg.

BODY

Row 1: Cut one strand of Orange leaving a long end for sewing. Holding one strand of Orange and one strand of Black together, work one row.

Rows 2-5 (Double wrap row)**:** Wrap each peg twice on wrapping row, and complete knit stitches by lifting bottom loop on each peg over the two new wraps and off the peg *(Figs. 7a & b, page 26 and 27)*. Lift each top wrap off the peg, making loose stitches *(Fig. 7c, page 27)* and pull work down from the inside to keep loops from slipping off the pegs.

Row 6 (Increase row)**:** Wrap empty peg on first side of work 3 times *(see Increases, page 25)*, wrap each peg twice, wrap next empty peg 3 times; complete same as previous row.

Continue to increase one stitch at **each** side, every other row, until 24{32-40} pegs are used.

Work in double wrap on 24{32-40} pegs until Body measures approximately 45{49-52}"/114.5{124.5-132} cm.

Decrease one stitch at **each** side, every other row, until 16{18-20} pegs are used *(see Decreases, page 25)*.

Work one row of single wrap.

CUFF

Cut Black. Holding two strands of Orange together, work in single wrap for 6" (15 cm).

Cut yarn leaving a long end for sewing.

Slip sts onto stitch holder, making sure yarn end is at the opening. Thread yarn with yarn needle.

To form Cuff, fold bottom edge to **wrong** side. Matching stitches, sew each stitch on stitch holder to each stitch on first row of Cuff.

With **wrong** side together, fold Shrug in half lengthwise; beginning at inside of Cuff, weave each Cuff and Body forming Sleeves, leaving the center 20{22-24}"/51{56-61} cm free *(Fig. 15, page 31)*.

Weave in all yarn ends; clip ends close to work.

Design by Charlene G. Finiello.

Wrap

■■■□ INTERMEDIATE

Finished Size: 14"h x 75"w (35.5 cm x 190.5 cm)

MATERIALS

- Bulky Weight Yarn **BULKY 5**
  [3½ ounces, 142 yards
  (100 grams, 129 meters) per skein]:
    2 skeins
- Bulky Weight Long Eyelash Yarn **BULKY 5**
  [1¾ ounces, 64 yards
  (50 grams, 58 meters) per skein]:
    2 skeins
- 41 Peg round wheel
- Knitting wheel tool
- Crochet hook
- Yarn needle

TIE

Holding one strand of each yarn together, make a flat piece on 5 pegs, 12" (30.5 cm) long **(see Flat Knitting, page 24)**.

BODY

Increase Row: Wrap each peg, wrap next empty peg twice **(see Increases, page 25)**; complete knit stitches: you will have 6 pegs used.

Work Increase Row every other row, until 30 pegs are used.

Work on 30 pegs for 9" (23 cm), ending at increased edge.

Decrease Row: Decrease **(see Decreases, page 25)**, wrap each peg; complete knit stitches.

Work Decrease Row every other row, until 5 pegs are left.

TIE

Work on 5 pegs for 12" (30.5 cm), ending on right hand side.

To work chain 1 bind off, insert crochet hook in loop on first peg and lift it off the peg, insert hook in loop on next peg, lift it off the peg and pull it through loop on hook, ★ chain 1 **(Fig. 13, page 30)**, insert hook in loop on next peg, lift it off the peg and pull it through loop on hook **(Fig. 8a, page 27)**; repeat from ★ until all of the loops have been removed from the wheel and there is one loop on crochet hook. Cut yarn and pull end through final loop **(Fig. 8c, page 27)**.

Weave in all yarn ends; clip ends close to work.

Design by Charlene G. Finiello.

Hat & Shawl

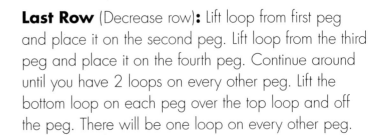

Hat: ◼◼◻◻ EASY
Shawl: ◼◼◼◻ INTERMEDIATE

Shawl Finished Size: 19″ x 58″ (48.5 cm x 147.5 cm)

MATERIALS

- Bulky Weight Nubby Yarn
  [1¾ ounces, 60 yards (50 grams, 55 meters) per skein]:
    4 skeins
- Bulky Weight Short Eyelash Yarn
  [1¾ ounces, 89 yards
  (50 grams, 82 meters) per skein]:
    3 skeins
- 36 Peg round wheel for Hat
- 41 Peg round wheel for Shawl
- Knitting wheel tool
- Yarn needle

HAT
CUFF

Using 36 peg wheel and holding one strand of each yarn together, make a tubular piece 1½″ (4 cm) long **(see Tubular Knitting, page 22)**.

To form Cuff, lift up bottom edge toward inside of wheel and place loops from first row over pegs **(Fig. 5, page 26)**. There will be 2 loops on each peg. Lift the bottom loop on each peg over the top loop and off the peg. Cuff is now secured in work and there is one loop on each peg.

BODY

Continue working for 7″ (18 cm).

Last Row (Decrease row)**:** Lift loop from first peg and place it on the second peg. Lift loop from the third peg and place it on the fourth peg. Continue around until you have 2 loops on every other peg. Lift the bottom loop on each peg over the top loop and off the peg. There will be one loop on every other peg.

Cut yarn leaving a 24″ (61 cm) end. Thread yarn needle with end. Beginning with the last peg, insert yarn needle in each loop and lift it off the peg **(Fig. 6a, page 26)**. With yarn to inside of Hat, pull the end tightly gathering the loops to the center of the tube **(Fig. 6b, page 26)**; knot yarn tightly and weave in the end; clip yarn close to work.

SHAWL

Row 1: Using 41 peg wheel and holding one strand of each yarn together, wrap 2 pegs and complete knit stitches **(see Flat Knitting, page 24)**.

Increase Row: Wrap each peg, wrap next empty peg twice **(see Increases, page 25)**; complete knit stitches: you will have 3 pegs used.

Work Increase Row every other row, until 41 pegs are used.

Work on 41 pegs for 4 rows, ending at increased edge.

Decrease Row: Decrease **(see Decreases, page 25)**, wrap each peg; complete knit stitches.

Work Decrease Row every other row, until 2 pegs are left.

Work on 2 pegs for 2 rows.

Last Row: Lift loop from first peg and place it on the second peg. Lift bottom loop over top loop and off the peg. Cut yarn and pull through loop on peg.

Weave in all yarn ends; clip ends close to work.

Design by Charlene G. Finiello.

General Instructions

ROUND WHEEL

> *Tip*   An easy project to make while learning how to use the knitting wheel is a simple tubular project such as the Ear Warmer, page 4, or Basic Hat, page 5.

WRAPPING THE YARN

Producing knit fabric on the wheels involves wrapping the yarn around the pegs. It is absolutely essential to wrap the yarn loose enough to be able to lift it off the peg, but not so loose that it falls off. As you wrap, let the yarn gently slide through your hand.

TUBULAR KNITTING

To create a tubular piece, work around and around on the round wheel, always working in the same direction. All of the pegs will be used.

> When instructed to **anchor yarn**, attach end of yarn to side peg with a slip knot **(Figs. 11a-c, page 30)**. This holds the beginning yarn and also the working yarn until you are ready to use it.

> *Tip*   If you are holding two or more strands of yarn together, be sure to treat them as one.

Step 1: Leaving a 6" (15 cm) end, insert yarn end in center of wheel from top to bottom, and anchor yarn **(Fig. 1a)**. Once anchored yarn is removed, the yarn end will hang to inside of wheel.

Fig. 1a

Step 2 (Foundation round)**:** Holding the wheel however it is most comfortable for you, wrap the yarn around the first peg (to the right of the anchored yarn) in a clockwise direction, ending at the inside of the wheel **(Fig. 1b)**. Moving around the wheel to your right and wrapping each peg loosely, wrap the next peg clockwise, ending at the inside. Continue around, turning the wheel every few wraps, and pushing the loops down with your other hand as you go until all of the pegs have been wrapped **(Fig. 1c)**.

> *Tip*   As you push the loops down, leave your finger on the last loop to prevent it from falling off.

Fig. 1b

Fig. 1c

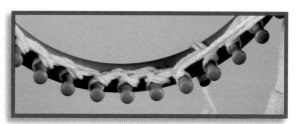
Fig. 1h

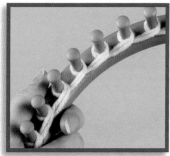
Fig. 1d

Fig. 1e

Step 5 (Wrapping round)**:** Wrap each peg clockwise, ending at the inside of the wheel (2 loops on each peg).

Step 6 (Completing knit stitches)**:** Using the tool and beginning with the last peg wrapped, lift the bottom loop on each peg over the top loop and off the peg.

Step 3: Continue around wrapping pegs clockwise a second time until all of the pegs have 2 loops on them, again pushing the loops down as you go *(Fig. 1f)*.

Note: After working 3 or 4 rounds, remove anchored yarn from side peg and allow bottom of piece to hang free.

Repeat Steps 5 and 6 for desired length.

The right side of the piece faces outward *(Fig. 1i)* and the wrong side faces inward. *(Fig. 1j)*.

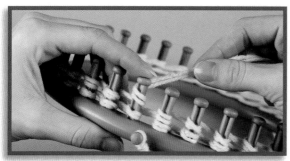
Fig. 1f

Note: If yarn has been wrapped too tightly, it will be very difficult to lift the bottom loop over the top loop (Step 4). If this is a problem, remove yarn and rewrap again, working looser.

Step 4: Using the tool, lift the bottom loop on the last peg wrapped over the top loop and off the peg *(Fig. 1g)*. This completes the knit stitch and secures the working yarn. Continue around working in either direction. Your first row of knitting is complete *(Fig. 1h)*.

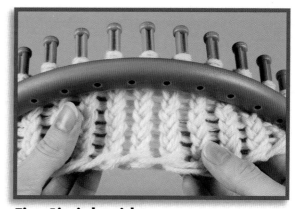
Fig. 1i right side

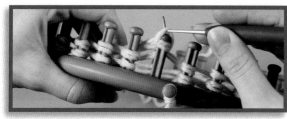
Fig. 1g

Fig. 1j wrong side

23

FLAT KNITTING

To create a flat piece, work back and forth on the round wheel instead of in a complete circle. All or only some of the pegs may be used.

> $\mathcal{T}ip$ It will be easier for you to learn flat knitting if you are familiar with tubular knitting first.

> $\mathcal{T}ip$ If you are holding two or more strands of yarn together, be sure to treat them as one.

Step 1: Leaving a 6" (15 cm) end, anchor yarn.

Step 2 (Foundation row)**:** Wrap the yarn around the first peg (to the right of the anchored yarn) in a clockwise direction, ending at the inside of the wheel **(Fig. 1b, page 22)**. Moving around the wheel to your right, continue to wrap the number of pegs required for your piece (clockwise), pushing the loops down with your other hand as you go.

> $\mathcal{T}ip$ The yarn should cross at the inside of the wheel, leaving a loop on the outside of each peg **(Figs. 1d & e, page 23)**.

Step 3: Wrap the last peg again clockwise **(Fig. 2a)**, then working to your left, wrap each peg counter-clockwise until all of the pegs have 2 loops on them **(Fig. 2b)**. Again the yarn should cross at the inside of the wheel.

Fig. 2a

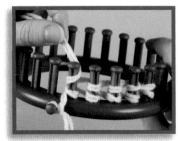

Fig. 2b

Step 4: Using the tool and beginning with the last peg wrapped **(Fig. 2c)**, lift the bottom loop on each peg over the top loop and off the peg, completing knit stitches **(Fig. 2d)**.

Fig. 2c

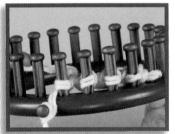

Fig. 2d

Step 5 (Wrapping row)**:** Wrap the first peg counter-clockwise **(Fig. 2e)**, then working to your right, wrap each remaining peg clockwise **(Fig. 2f)**.

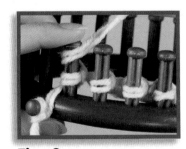

Fig. 2e

Fig. 2f

Step 6 (Completing knit stitches)**:** Using the tool and beginning with the last peg wrapped, lift the bottom loop on each peg over the top loop and off the peg.

Step 7 (Wrapping row)**:** Wrap the first peg clockwise, then working to your left, wrap each remaining peg counter-clockwise.

Step 8 (Completing knit stitches)**:** Using the tool and beginning with the last peg wrapped, lift the bottom loop on each peg over the top loop and off the peg.

> *Tip* There is an easy way to remember which direction to wrap the pegs on each row. The first peg is wrapped in the same direction as the last stitch on the previous row. The remaining pegs are wrapped in the opposite direction as the first peg.

Note: After working 3 or 4 rows, remove anchored yarn from side peg and allow bottom of piece to hang free.

Repeat Steps 5-8 for desired length, ending by working Step 6 or 8 **(Fig. 2g)**.

Fig. 2g

SHAPING ON FLAT KNITTING
INCREASES

On wrapping row, wrap empty peg twice on side of work to be increased **(Fig. 3)**. Complete the knit stitch by lifting the bottom loop over the top loop and off the peg. You will have one more peg being used for each increase made.

Note: When working in double wrap, wrap empty peg 3 times.

Fig. 3

DECREASES

On the side to be decreased, move the loop from the peg one stitch in from the edge to the peg at the edge, leaving an empty peg between them **(Fig. 4a)**. Insert the tool under both loops and move them to the empty peg **(Fig. 4b)**. This counts as the wrap. Wrap the remaining pegs and complete knit stitches. You will have one less peg being used at each decreased edge and the edge stitches will slant towards the inner stitches.

Fig. 4a

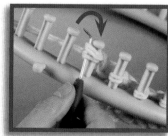

Fig. 4b

CHANGING OR ADDING YARN

Whether you are changing to a new color or adding an additional strand of yarn, anchor new yarn. Hold the new yarn by itself or together with the yarn to be added to, and begin wrapping. After working 3 or 4 rows with the new yarn, remove anchored yarn from side peg. When work is finished, the end can be brought to the wrong side and woven in to conceal it.

MAKING A CUFF

Make tubular piece as specified in instructions. To form a Cuff, lift up bottom edge toward inside of wheel and place loops from first row over pegs (*Fig. 5*). There will be 2 loops on each peg.

Lift the bottom loop on each peg over the top loop and off the peg. Cuff is now secured in work and there is one loop on each peg.

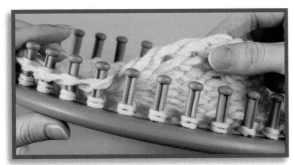

Fig. 5

REMOVING HAT FROM WHEEL

Cut yarn leaving a 24" (61 cm) end. Thread yarn needle with end. Beginning with the last peg, insert yarn needle in each loop and lift it off the peg (*Fig. 6a*).

With yarn to inside of Hat, pull the end tightly gathering the loops to the center of the tube (*Fig. 6b*); knot yarn tightly and weave in the end; clip end close to work.

Fig. 6a

Fig. 6b

DOUBLE WRAP

This versatile technique creates a loose stitch that is useful for making tams, shrugs and other items with a looser weave.

Begin with one or more rows of regular wrap.

Step 1: Wrap each peg twice on wrapping row or round (*Fig. 7a*). You will have 3 loops on each peg.

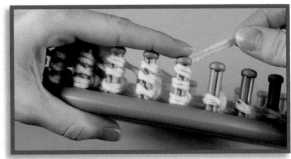

Fig. 7a

Step 2: Using the tool, lift the bottom loop on each peg over the two new wraps and off the peg **(Fig. 7b)**. There will be 2 loops on each peg.

Fig. 7b

Step 3: Lift each top wrap off the peg, making a loose stitch **(Fig. 7c)**. Pull bottom of work down to keep loops from slipping off the pegs.

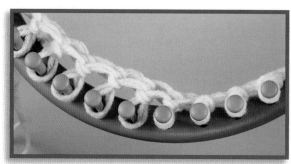

Fig. 7c

> *Tip* Steps 2 and 3 can be combined. Instead of working around the wheel twice, lift the bottom loop on the next peg over the two new wraps and off the peg, then lift the top wrap off the peg. Repeat for each peg. Be sure to pull bottom of work down as you go. Try both ways to see which you like better.

CHAIN ONE BIND OFF

Binding off is a process that removes the loops from the round wheel and secures the stitches.

Insert crochet hook in loop on last peg and lift it off the peg, working to your left, insert hook in loop on next peg, lift it off the peg and pull it through loop on hook **(Fig. 8a)**, ★ chain 1 **(Fig. 13, page 30)**, insert hook in loop on next peg, lift it off the peg and pull it through loop on hook; repeat from ★ **(Fig. 8b)** until all of the loops have been removed from the wheel and there is one loop on crochet hook. Cut yarn and pull end through final loop **(Fig. 8c)**; secure yarn.

Fig. 8a

Fig. 8b

Fig. 8c

STRAIGHT WHEEL

When instructed to **anchor yarn**, attach end of yarn to side peg with a slip knot **(Figs. 11a-c, page 30)**. This holds the beginning yarn and also the working yarn until you are ready to use it.

> *Tip* If you are holding two or more strands of yarn together, be sure to treat them as one.

Step 1: Holding the straight wheel horizontally in front of you and leaving a 6" (15 cm) end, insert yarn end in center of straight wheel from top to bottom and anchor yarn on outside peg on right hand side **(Fig. 9a)**. Once anchored yarn is removed, the yarn end will hang to inside of wheel.

Fig. 9a

Step 2 (Foundation row)**:** Wrap the yarn around the first peg on the top row in a clockwise direction **(Fig. 9b)** and around the bottom peg in a counter-clockwise direction **(Fig. 9c)**, forming a figure eight. Continue across, wrapping the yarn around the next peg on the top row in a clockwise direction and around the bottom peg in a counter-clockwise direction until all of the pegs needed have been wrapped, pushing the loops down as you go.

Fig. 9b

Fig. 9c

> *Tip* The yarn should cross at each peg at the inside of the wheel **(Fig. 9d)**, leaving a loop on the outside of each peg.

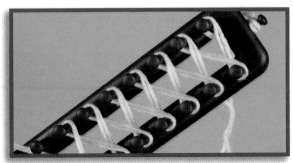

Fig. 9d

Step 3: Skip the last peg wrapped, as it will not be wrapped a second time. Move yarn straight up and wrap the yarn around the first peg on the top row counterclockwise **(Fig. 9e)**. Wrap the second peg on the bottom row clockwise **(Fig. 9f)**. Following the path of the yarn on foundation row, continue across, wrapping the yarn around the next peg on the top row in a counter-clockwise direction and around the bottom peg in a clockwise direction until all of the pegs have been wrapped, pushing the loops down as you go. There will be one loop on the skipped peg and 2 loops on all other pegs.

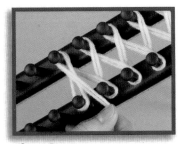

Fig. 9e

Fig. 9f

Note: If yarn has been wrapped too tightly, it will be very difficult to lift the bottom loop over the top loop (Step 4). If this is a problem, remove yarn and rewrap again, working looser.

Step 4: Using the tool, lift the bottom loop on the last peg wrapped over the top loop and off the peg **(Fig. 9g)**. This completes the stitch and secures the working yarn. Continue across both sides of the straight wheel. Your first row of knitting is complete **(Fig. 9h)**.

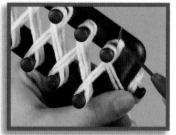

Fig. 9g

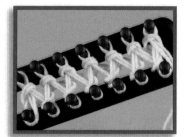

Fig. 9h

Note: Stitches will be loose and work will come down through center slot of wheel as work progresses.

Step 5 (Wrapping row)**:** Skip the last peg wrapped, as it will not be wrapped a second time. Working across the straight wheel from right to left, wrap the yarn around the first peg on the bottom row counter-clockwise. Wrap the second peg on the top row clockwise **(Fig. 9i)**. Following the path of the yarn on previous row, continue across, wrapping the yarn around the next peg on the bottom row in a counter-clockwise direction and around the top peg in a clockwise direction until all of the pegs have been wrapped, pushing the loops down as you go. There will be one loop on the first peg and 2 loops on all other pegs.

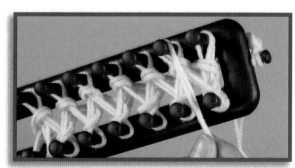

Fig. 9i

Step 6 (Completing stitches)**:** Using the tool and beginning with the last peg wrapped, lift the bottom loop on each peg over the top loop and off the peg.

To form remaining rows, skip the last peg wrapped and continue wrapping following figure 8 pattern established. There will be one loop on the first peg of each wrap sequence and 2 loops on all other pegs. Repeat Step 6 to complete the stitches **(Fig. 9j)**.

Fig. 9j

Note: After working 3 or 4 rows, remove anchored yarn from side peg and allow bottom of piece to hang free.

Chain 1 Bind off: Using a crochet hook, insert hook in loop on first peg and lift it off the peg, insert hook in peg straight across, lift it off the peg and pull it through loop on hook **(Fig. 10a)**, ★ chain 1 **(Fig. 13, page 30)**, insert hook in loop on next peg diagonally across, lift it off the peg and pull it through loop on hook, chain 1, insert hook in loop on next peg straight across, lift it off the peg and pull it through loop on hook; repeat from ★ until all of the loops have been removed from the wheel and there is one loop on crochet hook. Cut yarn and pull end through final loop **(Fig. 10b)**; secure yarn.

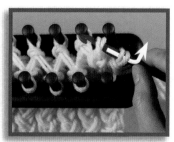

Fig. 10a

Fig. 10b

Symbols and Terms

★ – work instructions following ★ as many **more** times as indicated in addition to the first time.

working yarn – the strand coming from the skein

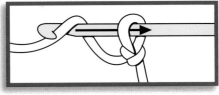

Yarn Weight Symbol & Names	SUPER FINE ①1	FINE ②2	LIGHT ③3	MEDIUM ④4	BULKY ⑤5	SUPER BULKY ⑥6
Type of Yarns in Category	Sock, Fingering, Baby	Sport, Baby	DK, Light Worsted	Worsted, Afghan, Aran	Chunky, Craft, Rug	Bulky, Roving
Knit Gauge Ranges in Stockinette St to 4" (10 cm)	27-32 sts	23-26 sts	21-24 sts	16-20 sts	12-15 sts	6-11 sts
Advised Needle Size Range	1-3	3-5	5-7	7-9	9-11	11 and larger

●□□□□ BEGINNER	Projects for first-time knitters using basic knit and purl stitches. Minimal shaping.
●■□□□ EASY	Projects using basic stitches, repetitive stitch patterns, simple color changes, and simple shaping and finishing.
●■■□□ INTERMEDIATE	Projects with a variety of stitches, such as basic cables and lace, simple intarsia, double-pointed needles and knitting in the round needle techniques, mid-level shaping and finishing.
●■■■□ EXPERIENCED	Projects using advanced techniques and stitches, such as short rows, fair isle, more intricate intarsia, cables, lace patterns, and numerous color changes.

Basic Crochet Stitches

SLIP KNOT

Make a circle and place the working yarn under the circle **(Fig. 11a)**. Insert the hook under the bar just made **(Fig. 11b)** and pull on both ends of the yarn to complete the slip knot **(Fig. 11c)**.

Fig. 11a

Fig. 11b

Fig. 11c

YARN OVER

Bring the yarn over the top of the hook from back to front, catching the yarn with the hook and turning the hook slightly toward you to keep the yarn from slipping off **(Fig. 12)**.

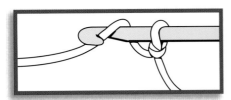

Fig. 12

CHAIN

Yarn over, draw the yarn through the loop on the hook **(Fig. 13)**.

Fig. 13

SLIP STITCH

Insert hook in stitch indicated, yarn over and draw through stitch and loop on hook **(Fig. 14)**.

Fig. 14

Finishing

WEAVING SEAMS

With the **right** side facing you and edges even, sew through both sides once to secure the seam. Insert the needle under the bar **between** the first and second stitches on the row and pull the yarn through (**Fig. 15**). Insert the needle under the next bar on the second side. Repeat from side to side, being careful to match rows.

Fig. 15

FRINGE

Cut a piece of cardboard 3" x 11" (7.5 cm x 28 cm). Wind the yarn **loosely** and **evenly** lengthwise around the cardboard until the card is filled, then cut across one end; repeat as needed.

Hold together as many strands as specified in individual instructions; fold in half.

With **wrong** side facing and using a crochet hook, draw the folded end up through a stitch and pull the loose ends through the folded end (**Fig. 16a**); draw the knot up **tightly** (**Fig. 16b**). Repeat, spacing as desired.

Fig. 16a

Fig. 16b

POM-POM

Cut a piece of cardboard 3" (7.5 cm) wide and as long as you want the diameter of your finished pom-pom to be.

Wind the yarn around the cardboard until it is approximately $1/2$" (12 mm) thick in the middle (**Fig. 17a**).

Carefully slip the yarn off the cardboard and firmly tie an 18" (45.5 cm) length of yarn around the middle (**Fig. 17b**). Leave yarn ends long enough to attach the pom-pom. Cut the loops on both ends and trim the pom-pom into a smooth ball (**Fig. 17c**).

Fig. 17a

Fig. 17b

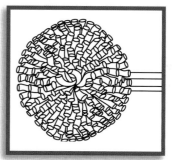

Fig. 17c

Yarn Information

The items in this leaflet were made using a variety of yarns. Any brand of the specified weight of yarn may be used. It is best to refer to the yardage/meters when determining how many balls or skeins to purchase. Remember, to achieve the same look, it is the weight of yarn that is important, not the brand of yarn.

For your convenience, listed below are the specific yarns used to create our photography models.

1. NECK CUFF & BELT
TLC® Macaroon™
White/Black - #9318 Salt & Pepper
Wal-Mart® Mainstay
Black - #1040 True Black

2. EAR WARMER
Patons® Divine
Blue - #06117 Denim Storm
Caron® Simply Soft Seasons
White - #2901 White

3. BASIC HAT
Wal-Mart® Mainstays
Black - #1040 Black
Red Heart® Fiesta®
Black/Gold - #6012 Black

4. SEQUINED HAT
Lion Brand® Jiffy
Color A - #153 Black
Patons® Allure
Color B - #04040 Ebony
Berroco® Mirror FX™
Color C - #9003 Gold/Black

5. SPIRIAL HAT
Wal-Mart® Mainstays
Black - #1040 True Black
Lion Brand® Wool-Ease®
White - #301 White/Multi

6. SHAGGY DOG HAT & SCARF
Bernat® Galaxy
Tan - #53011 Moon
Patons® Carmen
Off-White - #07008 Ivory

7. MOHAIR BAG
Lion Brand® Moonlight Mohair
Variegated - #204 Rainbow Falls
Hand spun Alpaca
Lt Brown

8. COTTON BAG
Red Heart® Casual Cot'n Blend™
#3578 Spice

9. SHRUG
Moda Dea™ Impact!™
Orange - #9263 Orange Crush
Moda Dea™ Now!™
Black - #9145 Black Diamond

10. WRAP
Patons® Divine
#06430 Richest Rose
Lion Brand® Fun Fur
#112 Raspberry

11. HAT & SHAWL
Bernat® Galaxy
#53134 Pluto
Red Heart® Foxy
#9353 Majesty